Dream Guidance

Interpret Your Dreams and
Create the Life You Desire!

Anna-Karin Bjorklund, M.A.

Bjorklund, Anna-Karin.

Dream guidance: interpret your dreams and create the life you desire!

ISBN-10: 0615730221; ISBN-13: 978-0615730226

Edited by Simone Gabbay

Images:
Cover: Atelier Sommerland/Shutterstock
p.25; 81: Cattallina/Shutterstock
p.48: Laschon Robert Paul/Shutterstock
p.85: Jessica Fiorini/Shutterstock
p.57;58 Max Sudakov/Shutterstock
p.61; 84; Anne Kitzman/Shutterstock
p.61 Daniela Barreto/Shutterstock
p.73 Migelito/Shutterstock
p.95 Microsoft Image Gallery
p.99: Sweet Lana/Shutterstock
p.114: Algol/Shutterstock
p.26; 42; 52; 62; 70; 78; 106; 118: Carla Castagno/Shutterstock
p.104 Swetlana Wall/Shutterstock
Author photo by Mia Falk

Disclaimer
No part of this book is intended to substitute for competent medical diagnosis or professional psychological services.

A dream which is not interpreted is like a letter which is not read.

The Talmud

Contents

To all dreamers around the world.

Introduction

Dreams are wonderful in so many ways! They not only help clear unconscious emotional blockages and enhance our awareness, but miraculously also guide us with beautiful messages, premonitions, and unique wisdom. The adventures we embark on during our nightly dream voyages can feel as real as events out of an ordinary day, or as remote and foreign as though we were in a different time and place altogether. Some dreams help us with just the right guidance needed at a particular point in time. Other dreams help us foresee events in the future that we could never have predicted in waking life, or we may even dream about an event happening simultaneously in another part of the world. Yet we are still inside our mind the whole time...or are we...?

Even though most of our dreams relate to our own personal circumstances, we sometimes dream about life issues, situations, people, or maybe even places or dimensions we have never heard about. Or we get urgent premonitions that don't relate to our own life in any way. If we were truly inside our own mind the whole night, how could we possibly receive all this information? According to the late Swiss psychiatrist Carl Jung, when we dream, we tap into the collective unconscious.[1] Jung described the collective unconscious as a shared field that connects us all, even beyond the limits of time and space. This field can also be likened to the notion of an astral plane, or the Eastern understanding of an underlying Tao.

Even if you don't always remember your dreams, you can probably think of at least a few occasions when you woke up and couldn't help but wonder why you just had such a strange dream. We often draw on material from the astral plane or the collective unconscious to help make sense of our own lives, and sometimes we even get insights that stretch our understanding of the Universe!

As a lifelong dreamer and devoted dream worker, I have studied the dream theories of Carl Jung, Sigmund Freud, and Edgar Cayce, along with those of many other spiritual teachers around the world. One thing that I have found through my extensive research, analysis of other people's dreams, and, last but not least, from my own nightly journeys into the dream realms, is that we may never know exactly what a dream is trying to tell us, or what it means. Dreams are highly complex and filled with multi-dimensional interpretation possibilities.

In contrast to the more generic dream books and dictionaries often seen on bookstore shelves, the dream interpretations in this book combine intuitive sciences with Jungian psychology and emphasize the importance of feelings, associations, and dream context, while also inviting guidance and premonitions from the astral realms. You will learn how to categorize the type of dream that you had and see how can you work with any type of dream by following an easy step-by-step approach, asking the dream specific questions (see chapters 3 and 8).

Thousands of Years of Dreams and Inspiration

The interest in dreams is by no means new. There are documentations of dreams reaching back thousands of years. In ancient Greece, they had dream temples dedicated to dream healing and receiving sacred messages from the gods. Native Americans placed high values on their dreams as well. Some Iroquois tribes even believed a person could get very sick if dreams were ignored.[2] As we will see in the chapter about nightmares, they were right about the importance of dreams. If we ignore our dreams, emotional blockages are built up and we do indeed risk becoming very sick. Many world religions also honor dreams. In the Bible, there are over a hundred references to dreams, and many Tibetan Buddhists practice dream yoga, a beautiful way of enhancing higher states of awareness even when dreaming.

Australian aborigines believe in the concept of "Dreamtime," the space where everything is created and dreamed. According to this tradition, we dream ourselves into this world, and then back into Dreamtime! The Australian aborigines' view on dreams illustrates that there is, in fact, no differentiation between past, present, and future. It is all happening now, in Dreamtime. In the chapters about synchronicity and guidance, we will see that we can miraculously dream about something that is simultaneously happening in another part of the world, or dream of a person we haven't seen in years, only for them to show up on our doorstep the next day! The concepts of time and space may not be as fixed as we believe them to be.

Many scientists and fiction authors have also drawn inspiration from their dreams. For instance, author Robert Louis Stevenson dreamed up the story of Dr. Jekyll and Mr. Hyde in one of his dreams, and the Russian chemist Dmitri Mendeleev received help from his dreams when he discovered the right order of the elements according to their atomic weight.[3]

Dreams and Psychology

Both Sigmund Freud and Carl Jung integrated dream analysis into their analytical work with clients, and saw dreams as a vital component of psychological growth and health. Jung's contributions to dream psychology came to be even more encompassing than Freud's, and he developed a much broader spiritual understanding of dreams and the connectedness between us all. Jung's dream concepts have not only been integrated into many of today's psychological theories, but also form the backbone of many spiritual and self-growth schools of thoughts.

In my own dream work with clients, I place high importance on dreams, both from a psychological and spiritual perspective. We spend about a third of our lives sleeping, and perhaps as much as half of our lives (or more!) in unconscious states, and as dreams are a direct expression of the unconscious, they can indeed reveal many hidden aspects of our personalities and life situations that we are not yet aware of. Therefore, if we were to just look at what we think we are experiencing in our daily lives, but ignore what is happening in our dreams, we would miss out on highly valuable information! By listening to our dreams, we integrate all aspects of ourselves and are able to form a more complete picture.

It is also important to remember that our egos represent only a small component of our total selves, and as a consequence, what we are aware of (our ego) will always have just a partial view of life because of limited consciousness, so the importance of dreams cannot be emphasized enough. By looking closer at your dreams, you not only learn more about what is really going on in your life, but you also develop new attitudes and perspectives on situations. You may, for example, not be aware of feeling upset about something, but then a dream helps shed light on the issue, and instead of forming an emotional blockage, you are now able to clear it out by processing the situation.

Dreams and Intuition

The guidance, intuitive insights, and mysterious journeys we embark on to far-away realms may indeed be the most exciting part of dreaming! Our dream adventures and encounters can be miraculous, and offer us immense guidance and support. Other types of dreams come with strong premonitions about events that are about to happen, or they give you deeper insights into certain situations in your life. You can fine-tune your intuition and ability to better read the messages in your dreams by being extra alert in your daily life and paying close attention to situations that remind you about something you have dreamt of. In this way, you become even more receptive to the messages coming your way, even in your outer world. Dream symbols do not stop when we wake up; rather, the energy of dreams actually continues throughout the day. By also becoming more observant of the world around us, we will find that symbols that remind us of images from our inner dream world begin to appear all over the place! When our inner and outer worlds collaborate to create messages for us, we are experiencing meaningful coincidences, also known as *synchronicity*. We will return to this beautiful form of guidance later in the book.

Dreams and Affirmations

When you listen to your dreams, emotional reactions and situations you may not yet be aware of rise to the surface, and this process helps clear out the dissonance that so often occurs when you are having an unconscious reaction to situations in life. You may have a deep underlying feeling that clashes with an unconscious reaction and end up feeling overwhelmed without even knowing why, or how. If you don't process your reactions, emotional blockages are created, and they trap and weigh you down, and actually make it much more difficult to manifest and affirm positive developments in your life. In those situations, even if you were to think positive thoughts, there is not enough space to stay positive because the negative weight would pull you down.

Dream work helps you develop a much better understanding of your true underlying feelings, and by helping you see what is really going on in your life, emotional blockages are released. With all this new space, you now have the room you need to attract more positive thoughts into your daily life, and to remain positive. When you are able to stay on a higher frequency, you now begin to build a unique tool kit—the power to create the life you desire!

When we know what we really want, and the energy is flowing, we begin to resonate on that level, and we are now choosing the thoughts that are serving us in the best possible way. Dreams help us embark on our true paths, and fill us with the energy we need to continue in the right direction. We become more receptive to the guidance from our higher self and develop the power to create our dream life!

Chapter 1

AN INTRODUCTION TO DREAM REALMS, INSPIRED BY JUNGIAN PSYCHOLOGY

The world of dream psychology is a fascinating place. Many different schools of psychology today embrace and invite dreams into the therapy room. Even though there are many excellent dream researchers and thinkers around, any dream book would be incomplete without reference to both Sigmund Freud and Carl Jung.

Sigmund Freud and Carl Jung

Both Sigmund Freud and Carl Jung played significant roles in the development of depth psychology and even though they differed in their approach, they both placed high emphasis on dreams. Sigmund Freud is often referred to as the father of psychoanalysis, and he did indeed contribute significantly to the field of dream psychology by introducing us to the concept of the unconscious and the importance of dreaming. Carl Jung was Freud's student, and, as we will see in this book, he came to develop an even broader understanding of dreams with a higher emphasis on the spiritual dimensions. Freud may have called dreams "the royal road to the unconscious," but, in contrast to Jung, Freud used dreams primarily to help his patients become aware of their repressed sexual desires, which, according to Freud, were at the root of all neurotic disturbances.[1] Whereas Freud viewed dreams as wish fulfillments and very much related them to suppressed sexuality, Jung viewed dreams as a product of our total psyche, i.e., as not only as coming from our personal unconscious, but rather as also having major influences from the collective unconscious, the field shared by all of us, and also as helping us form more complete perspectives and become better as individuals.[2]

Many of the concepts discussed in this book are inspired by Jung's wonderful dream teachings. In this chapter, we will therefore look at some of Jung's remarkable contributions to the world of depth psychology, and see how Jung built a beautiful foundation to the understanding of our dreams. We will begin with the powerful concept of the collective unconscious, which, spiritually, can be compared to some of the dimensions found in the astral plane. It is indeed the backbone of much of Jungian dream psychology and helps us understand how it is possible for us to tap into so much information just by sleeping!

The Collective Unconscious (The Astral Plane)

Thought of by many people today as the astral plane, Jung referred to this majestic field that connect us all and is present within all living beings, as the collective unconscious.[3] This is the field we tap into when we dream, and it is of particular interest in both intuitive approaches to dreams and Jungian depth psychology, as it shows how dreams, coincidences, and symbolic connections do not always originate within our personal unconscious, but also in this connected energy field, hence explaining how we can sometimes dream of events to which we have no connection in any way in our daily lives.

Jung was one of the pioneers of this concept, and often talked about how many of his inspirations came from this unconscious realm. He said it is because we visit this field when we dream that our dreams sometimes bring about ideas or symbols that are totally foreign to our own personal lives, but may have been of significance to humanity at some other point in time.[4] This concept brings some clarity into how we sometimes dream of something very abstract and symbolic, such as a dragon or a sacred scripture, without ever having consciously experienced anything of that nature in our own lives. Or we may dream about some event that was influenced by a myth from another part of the world, but that was somehow "translated" into a situation that made more sense to us. We may also have a premonition about an event that hasn't even happened yet, or would have been impossible for us to foresee in waking life. These types of experiences really show the significance of this interrelated field, and how connected we all really are. We will revisit these types of phenomena later in the book in the chapters about synchronicity and intuition.

Our Psyche

In the Jungian school of thought, our psyche has four dimensions.[5] In the middle of our psyche is the archetype of Self. The Self is the regulating center of the *entire psyche* and helps us feel whole.[6] It is commonly referred to today as our higher self. Our ego, on the other hand, is only at the centre of our *personal consciousness*, i.e., not the entire psyche. It is important to make a strong note here that our ego is only conscious of what is within our personal consciousness, which further highlights the value of dreams, as they help enhance the flow between our unconscious and conscious parts, and bring higher awareness of both our inner and outer worlds.

Personal Dimension

> *Personal consciousness* includes content of which we are aware. The ego is at the centre of the personal consciousness.

The personal unconscious is comprised of content that is personal to us, but is currently forgotten or repressed.

Collective Dimension

The collective consciousness relates to the cultural values that have been built up and shared over time, and are now shared by all humans.

The collective unconscious is a field that is shared by all living beings, and that exists beyond both time and space. In Jungian psychology, the collective unconscious comprises the archetypes, the universal patterns of behavior that influence us with their energy patterns.[7] Depending on our upbringing and culture, archetypal images and themes are revealed to us in our dreams in a way that makes sense to us. That's why there are many fairy tales around the world that are based on similar principles, but feature different story characters. It is also the reason why many of our dreams are similar in nature, such as being chased by a monster, or nurtured by a mother. An archetype that often shows up in dreams is the Wise Old Man. The specific archetypal image of the Wise Old man will vary, depending on the culture in which he shows up. A

Hindu may see him as a guru, whereas a Christian may see him as a certain saint, and a Buddhist as a monk or as Buddha himself. Whether we call it the astral plane or the collective unconscious, it is a fascinating field filled with universal wisdom. Best of all—we tap into it every night when we sleep!

Individuation

Perhaps of most significance in all of Jung's psychological concepts when it comes to dream work is the process of *individuation*. Individuation allows us to grow and become all that we can be. Because the unconscious is so enormous, it may not be possible to achieve full individuation, at least not while we are alive, as we will always have some aspect of ego present within us, and the ego is only conscious of our personal consciousness. Jung said that the importance does not lie in the amount of the achievement, but rather in being on the path itself![8] Listening to our dreams is a vital function of the path of individuation, as individuation involves a beautiful dialogue between our ego and our higher self. The term "the transcendent function" refers to an enhanced flow between our unconscious and conscious side, and this communication is enhanced when we work with our dreams.[9]

It is our higher self that directs our dreams and sends

messages and insights to our conscious part. The symbols in our dreams are carefully selected from all dimensions of our psyche, including the collective unconscious, to best get the message across. The more we work out our emotional imbalances, the more receptive we become to the higher guidance that is available to us. We can then spend more of our dream time tapping into miraculous wisdom, and become the best we can possibly be!

Jung's Inspirations

Much of dream psychology as we know it today was inspired by Jung and his remarkable theories. Jung introduced the world to some magnificent and highly insightful concepts, inspired by many different areas, including Romantic philosophy, depth psychology, religion, alchemy, and mysticism.

Jung was also strongly influenced by his mother's interest and experiences in the paranormal, and also experienced many paranormal events of his own, which he writes about in his autobiography *Memories, Dreams, Reflections*.[10] It was Jung's mother who introduced him to Eastern religions, and he studied Hindu yogic traditions, Zen Buddhism, Taoism, and Tibetan teachings.

In his memoir, Jung shared how he particularly appreciated the Eastern way of placing emphasis on the inner life, rather than the outer. Jung's wonderful approach to our psyche and the world around us is a major influencer behind many psychological theories, and forms the basis of many of the concepts shared in this book.

Chapter 2

DECODE MESSAGES FROM YOUR DREAM CHARACTERS

Although intuitive guidance dreams and premonitions may sometimes be about humanity as a whole, most of your dreams are unique to yourself and are primarily concerned with you! Because your own personal experiences play such a crucial role in each dream, it is always going to be difficult for even the most seasoned dream analyst to correctly interpret your dreams. That being said, there are some universal dream themes that we all share from time to time, and we will look at some popular dream interpretation examples together later in this book. The most important part of dream interpretation is seeing how the associations you make with dream images relate to your life right now. The examples provided in the dream interpretation guide in chapter 8 have been chosen carefully, with a specific set of questions suggested around each dream theme to help you as you develop your own dream interpretation process.

To assist you in building a better understanding of how to best work with your dreams, this chapter introduces you to some of the most central aspects of dreaming: dreams of ourselves, others, and unknown people.

Dreams of Ourselves and Others – Our Persona and Shadow

Dreams are multidimensional and can bring many types of messages for us, from both subjective and objective angles. As we will see in the next chapter, there are also intuitive forms and even astral types of dreams! On the subjective level, dreams revolve around your own inner drama, and the dream figures in subjective dreams have actually been chosen to represent unknown aspects of yourself. On the objective level, dream figures may instead have been chosen to help highlight an interaction that is currently going on between you and other people in your life, or to help you gain insight about your relationships with others. Almost all our dreams feature some type of character. As a general rule of thumb, most dreams are subjective, and the figures in our dream represent a part of ourselves (even when we dream of people we know). Each person in a subjective dream has been chosen very carefully to highlight something that is also present within us. We will look at subjective and objective types of dreams in more detail in the next chapter.

The Persona

We all have different aspects of our personality within us, and by developing a better understanding of ourselves and the roles we play in the outer world, it becomes much easier to see what the dream is trying to tell us. Two well-known Jungian concepts are our *persona* and our *shadow*. These aspects are important as they illustrate how we present ourselves to the world (our persona or mask) and what we are hiding (our shadow).[1] Do you know which side of yourself you present to others in different situations? When we are connected to our higher self and there is a healthy flow within our psyche, our persona will be well balanced. There are certain situations that require us to adapt to society slightly differently, depending on what we are doing. For example, there are many social roles that carry certain expectations, both from ourselves and from those around us, such as mother, father, wife, husband, doctor, police officer, etc. As we develop our ego, we choose various persona roles and integrate them into our ego-identity.

If we put too much of our energy into our persona, or our outer roles in life, we may feel empty, as though there were no real person inside us. In those situations, our ego is no longer governed by our higher self, but rather we now place too much emphasis on our outer roles. We are imbalanced! For example, a businessman who stays working late in the office every night, likely feels empty when he is not working. He has over-identified with his corporate role, and lacks a true sense of identity. On the other hand, if we do not develop our persona in a sufficient manner, we easily become hurt by even the smallest situations. We need to have some structure in different settings. So again, there needs to be a balance!

The Shadow

Awareness is indeed the key in any type of self-growth, and our dreams are here to help us. Perhaps of even more importance, when it comes to identifying different aspects of ourselves, is the part that we are not aware of at all! In addition to having a persona, we also have a shadow,[2] which is the part of ourselves that we are not only hiding from ourselves, but also from others (although others are more likely to see it than we are!). The shadow contains aspects of ourselves that we have unconsciously repressed, either because we did not like those traits, or because we thought others did not like them. Our shadow is often personified in dream characters, and is also projected onto people in our daily life and surrounding environment. By working with the projections we make onto other people or objects in our dreams, we can get a better understanding of our own shadow.

For example, we may project our shadow onto someone we dislike or envy onto a dream character, and by analyzing the characters in our dreams, we often see that they have qualities that are also present within ourselves that we may not yet be conscious of!

Dreams of Unknown Men and Women—Our Anima and Animus

Sometimes the people in our dreams are total strangers, and an unknown man or woman may even be taking center stage. Again, it is important to remind ourselves that most characters that enter our dream world have been carefully chosen to highlight something going on with us.

The unknown man or woman often represents the feminine and masculine aspects within ourselves. The Jungian terms for these archetypal forces are *anima* and *animus*. You may have come across these terms in everyday discussions with associates at work, with friends, or even in popular magazines.

The anima is the feminine archetype within a man, and the animus is the masculine archetype within a woman.[3] We tend to project our anima/animus on people of the opposite sex. When we are experiencing this type of projection, we may feel that we have fallen in love, and we often feel rather fascinated by those on whom we project our anima/animus image!

Although anima/animus projection often begins with mesmerizing and idealization, it can easily turn into disgust and annoyance, as we see parts of ourselves that we don't like, and that is when our shadow emerges! Being aware of this type of projection as it shows up in our dreams can protect us from pain and tears later on. True love is not a projection, but a constant state of being.

By working with all aspects of ourselves, and continuously turning to our dreams, we develop a much higher awareness of ourselves, which reduces the risks of becoming lost in this projection process. The feminine and male sides of ourselves are often in conflict, and they are always trying to achieve perfect harmony. Dreams of an unknown man or an unknown woman can help you see how well you are balancing your energies, and whether or not you are utilizing them both to your highest potential.

If you are a woman and dream of an unknown man, it may be your animus, or masculine part of yourself, that is showing up. Your masculine side represents the autonomous part of yourself, and the ability to be assertive, and go after what you want. If the unknown man is being nice to you, or if you are making love, this could signify that you are doing a good job integrating your male energies into your life right now. If you are being chased by an unknown man, you may be running away from your masculine qualities, and you may need to stand your ground a bit more, and become more autonomous!

If you are a man and dream of an unknown woman, this may be your anima, or feminine side of yourself. Your feminine side represents your ability to be more receiving, caring, intuitive, and even philosophical. If the woman in the dream is weak or vulnerable, it may mean that you need to strengthen your feminine side. It could also be a message for you to listen more to your intuition. Jung's notion of anima and animus really helps bring more clarity about why we so often encounter an unknown man or woman in our dreams.

Dreams truly have the potential to help bring awareness of all aspects of ourselves, and we not only develop higher self-knowledge and a healthier connection with our higher self, but we also release emotional blockages in the process. Best of all, when we listen to our dreams, we become more open to our own miraculous guidance, and blossom into our authentic selves!

Dreams are today's answers to tomorrow's questions.

Edgar Cayce

Chapter 3

AN INTUITIVE STEP-BY-STEP GUIDE TO DREAM
INTERPRETATION

Dreams can be very puzzling and confusing! It is no wonder we sometimes feel overwhelmed from not being able to "make sense" of our dreams. We may even brush them away as nonsense. Whatever type of dream you are having, they all provide you with powerful guidance one way or the other. All types of dreams are valuable, not only the "big" ones! Even the "little" dreams help in some form. Even if you are not receiving guidance in the form of premonitions or insightful messages in a dream, it doesn't mean you are not growing. The dream may instead be helping you emotionally and allowing you to process unconscious emotional feelings and reactions.

Symbolic Language

Your journeys to the dream realms are filled with adventures designed to help you along the way. By taking the time to work with your dreams and interpret the symbols, you can find helpful messages in the most unexpected places.

There are a couple of points to remember before we proceed with the actual dream interpretation process:

1. Dreams are not made up of the same language we use in our daily lives. The dream world relies on a more *symbolic language*, which is made up of images that have been carefully selected by our unconscious selves to communicate something important to us. Because dreams are symbolic by nature, they are not linear in any way. That is why we often feel confused by all the different scenes!

2. Dreams are *multidimensional*, and there is no "one-size-fits-all" type of interpretation approach, such as those found in dream dictionaries. If, for example, you know someone whose thumb has been amputated, and then dream about a hand where the thumb is missing, the associations you make with such an image will be very different from someone else's. Likewise, you may dream about an ocean, but how you felt when you looked at the ocean is equally important. If you felt frightened by the ocean, it will have a whole different meaning than it would if you felt inspired by it. Dream dictionaries can be useful first resources, but they will often provide you with only one possible association, when in reality, you may have a very different personal association that is much more fitted to your life situation. That being said, there are certain common dream themes that are often shared among all of us, such as falling, going back to school, being chased, etc. We will look at some of these dreams later in the book and see how you can

use these examples in your own dream interpretation process.

The context in which the dream occurs can also give you many clues. Ask yourself, "What is the relevance of the dream in my life right now?" "How did the dream make me feel?" "Where in my life do I feel like that?"

Dream Interpretation Steps

The dream interpretation steps below have been developed from years of extensive dream research, and from working with countless interpretations of clients' dreams, both from an intuitive and psychological perspective, and last but not least, from my own nightly dream voyages. The steps offer an intuitive approach to dreams, while also integrating the Jungian process of making associations and amplifying symbols to see how the associations best fit into your life right now.[1]

Step 1: Write the Dream in Your Dream Journal!

The insights that come from writing down your dreams cannot be emphasized enough. Writing is a transformative process that helps connect our inner and outer worlds in a very symbolic way. When you write down the dream, reflect upon:

Who is in the dream?

Where is it taking place?

What is happening?

What is the outcome?

What are you thinking?

What are you feeling?

Step 2: Categorize Your Dream—What Type of Dream Is It?

Dreams typically fall in one of four main categories: Subjective (projection), objective (processing of feelings), intuitive (guidance), and astral (visits). Popular subsets of dream categories include wish dreams, lucid dreams, recurrent dreams, and nightmares. Knowing what type of dream you are working with helps you immensely in the dream interpretation process.

Dream Type 1 – The Subjective Dream: *Know Thyself!*

Most of our dreams are subjective in one way or the other in that they are designed to help enhance our self-knowledge while also helping us process our emotions and feelings. In a subjective dream, the dream characters represent different parts of you and have been carefully chosen to highlight qualities that are also present within you. In other words, you are projecting aspects of yourself onto characters in the dream so that you can more easily see that these qualities are also within you! If an angry man is chasing you in your dreams, think about what you may be running away from. Perhaps you feel frightened by your own aggressive behaviors. You may not even be aware of what you are hiding. These types of dreams are helpful tools for finding out and learning more about yourself. As a general rule of thumb, when there is something slightly different about the people in your dream from their "ordinary" appearance in daily life, they have probably been chosen to represent certain qualities within you, so think about what stands out about the characters. What comes to mind when you think of this person? How do their actions in the dream remind you about yourself?

Dream Type 2 – The Objective Dream:
Relationship with Others and Emotional Processing

Sometimes dreams are more objective in nature and can indeed be about the other person, or rather the relationship you have with that person. In an objective dream, the dream characters have entered your dream as themselves and have been chosen to highlight the interaction, communication, and issues between you. The characters could also have been chosen to help you process different emotional reactions and underlying feelings. If, for example, you are having an argument with your partner, the dream could be helping you to better understand how you feel about a certain situation and help you see the situation from different perspectives. By letting the feelings come to the surface, you also release energetic blockages.

Dream Type 3 – The Intuitive, Prophetic, or Synchronistic Dream:
Intuitive Guidance to Help You Prepare for Life Events or Guide You in a Certain Direction

Intuitive dreams are designed to help guide you in a particular direction and may also give you urgent messages. The process of receiving information while dreaming is popularly known as telepathic dreaming. However, all intuitive dreams are not telepathic, as the information does not necessarily need to be conveyed by another person. Rather, most messages in intuitive dreams are delivered by your higher self. As a general rule, if the dream has a good "sequence," i.e., the scenes more or less follow a story line and don't feel as confusing as other dreams, or if you feel as though you're "observing" the dream, rather than participating in it, and you have no major emotional reactions, it could be a premonition or intuitive guidance dream, so pay close attention!

Synchronistic dreams miraculously bring together images, symbols, or events from your inner world (such as a dream image) with a corresponding event or symbol in your outer world. Such powerful coincidences help guide you in the right direction, and they also show how there is no real separation between our inner and outer worlds.

Dream Type 4- The Astral Dream:
Help from Your Guides and Visits to Other Realms

Along with synchronistic and prophetic dreams, astral dreams also help us understand that we may not always be "inside our minds" at night, but that we sometimes take actual journeys into other realms. Again, we can see how the separation between the different night realms may not be as clear as we first think. In these types of dream journeys, you may visit faraway places, fairylands, historical venues, or even the life of someone who lived hundreds of years ago. You may meet with deceased relatives and friends, angels, spirit guides, and other astral beings. Dragons, mermaids, and fairies often show up in astral dreams as well. Astral dreams offer powerful guidance and unique wisdom. As we saw in the earlier chapters about Jungian psychology, the notion of a collective unconscious fits hand in hand with the dimensions we visit in astral dreams. Often, astral journeys are lucid, which means that you are fully conscious of dreaming, while dreaming!

Dream Sub-Categories

Most of our dreams can fit into one of the four major types of dream categories discussed above. There are some dream themes that fit very well into any of the above categories, depending on the situation and feelings experienced. Other times, the dream themes detailed below form new categories altogether!

The Wish-Fulfillment Dream

What would we do without wish-fulfillment dreams! These miraculous night voyages can fill us with the sense that we can achieve, get, and be anything we want. The power of a clear mind, without doubt and worry, is immensely powerful. When you can learn how to capture the confidence that comes from such dreams, the world is your oyster! We will revisit this concept in chapter 9.

The Lucid Dream

To be lucid when dreaming means that you are actually aware of that you are dreaming, while still dreaming! Lucid dreams sometimes happen spontaneously, and we often wake up as soon as we realize we are dreaming. However, with practice, you can actually learn to remain sleeping, and even invite more lucid dreams. By testing yourself a few times throughout the day to see if you are dreaming you can bring this consciousness into the dream world as well. You can, for example, try to take an extra high jump up in the air and see what happens, or pinch yourself in the arm and see if you feel anything.

The Recurrent Dream

Some dreams come back around! Recurrent dreams sometimes come about to help you see something that is going on, but which you are unable to see for some reason. They can also relate to an event that happened to you a long time ago. If so, the reason a dream is coming back is likely because you are still reliving the same pattern, and the dream is here to help you see it. Recurring dreams are very important, as they really highlight something that is going on and is possibly even being recreated over and over because we have not yet worked it out.

Recurrent dreams are most often subjective, i.e., they concern something going on within you, but sometimes they can also be objective in that they highlight patterns you're recreating with others. They can occasionally also be both intuitive and astral in nature, for instance if you're not listening to the messages revealed to you, although these types of recurrent dreams are less common.

The Nightmare

A nightmare is a desperate cry for attention from your higher self. You are not getting the message, so the dream has now turned into something incredibly strong and terrifying to ensure that you are listening. The nightmare is not your enemy, but rather you friend! Nightmares come about to help us heal, by highlighting very urgent situations that we need to attend to.

In contrast to guidance dreams, which rarely evoke any emotions, nightmares evoke intense emotional reactions within us. They can be both subjective and objective, and often revolve around unprocessed feelings and emotions. They may also highlight particular situations that are damaging in our lives. As we will discuss further in chapter 5, they can also be astral.

Step 3: Make Associations with Dream Symbols and Characters

Now that you have identified what type of dream you have been in, you can continue exploring the symbols in your dream and see what associations come to mind. Your unconscious has chosen each symbol in the dream for a reason, so it is very important to reflect upon what you personally associate each symbol, event, or feeling with! For example, if you dreamt of a dolphin in the water, write down details about what a dolphin means to you, and what you associate water with. Remember to go back to each dream image in this exercise, i.e., make associations from each image or event; do not continue with a "free association." A free association would be when you first make an association with water, and then continue to associate that association with something else. It is better to work with the original image, as, after all, that is what your unconscious self has chosen to communicate something to your conscious self.

Step 4: How Does Your Dream Relate to Your Life Right Now?

Think about what is happening in your life. Ask yourself how such a dream came about, and what experiences you had the previous day. Take note of the context of each feeling or image in the dream. Do you see any similarities between the associations with the dream images and events in your current life?

Subjective Dream

If it is a subjective dream, how is the dream highlighting some unknown or repressed aspect about yourself?

Objective Dream

If it is an objective dream, is the dream helping you better deal with a situation by processing your feelings? Or is it maybe giving you another perspective? What is going on in your life right now, and why did this dream come just now?

Intuitive Dream

How are you feeling in the dream? If you are not having any major emotional reaction and the story line is pretty coherent, it could be an intuitive dream. Are you being called to pay extra attention to some events that are happening, or about to happen? How could these insights be of help to you right now? Pay close attention to anything that is being revealed to you in the dream!

Astral Dream

If it is an astral dream and you're being visited by deceased relatives, spirit guides, or beings from other realms, what is the message for you? Why did they come to you now? You may also have tapped into some sacred universal wisdom in a very special dream journey or initiation. Treasure your astral dreams; they are worth gold!

Wish-Fulfillment Dream

Wish fulfillment dreams tend to occur at moments in time when you need a little extra push and maybe an encouraging pat on the shoulder. How can you relive the powerful feeling of having your wish came true in the dream? Wish dreams can also help you heal from not being able to get what you wish for in your daily life, and instead let you experience having it come true in your dreams. The actual scenario in the dream is not as important as the feeling of having your wishes fulfilled!

Lucid Dream

Lucid dreams are exceptionally powerful in that you can use your conscious mind when interpreting them, and you often have some type of ability to change the course of direction in the dream, which helps you practice the power of positive thinking!

Recurrent Dream

What is the message you are not getting? Or do you already know what the issue is, but hope it will go away? Until you have sorted out the situation, your dreams will come back in recurrent form, and they may even develop into different story lines with the same theme as they try to highlight the issue from new angles.

Nightmare

If you don't listen to the messages in your "regular" dreams, or work out the issues in recurrent dreams, your dreams can quickly escalate into nightmares. Nightmares are a serious cry for help, so it is very important that you pay close attention to these dreams and see why they have come about. We'll return to nightmares in chapter 5.

Enrich Your Life!

Whatever type of dream you are having, remember you are having this dream at this particular moment in time for a reason! The more you work with your dreams, the more you will start seeing themes and messages shining through also in your daily life. Write down as many dreams you can remember each morning, and keep at it! By looking at dreams as a series, you can see how they change over time. Keep your dreams alive, and look back in your dream journal from time to time. When you come across something in your daily life that reminds you of a dream image, add those experiences as notes in your journal as well. As you enhance your awareness, you become more receptive to the guidance both in your dreams and outer world. By adding corresponding events from your daily life, as well as any other insights that may come to mind, to your dream journal, your dreams will be enriched, or, as

Jung would say "amplified," and you never know where this beautiful process will take you![1]

Every great dream begins with a dreamer. Always remember,
you have within you the strength, the patience, and the passion
to reach for the stars to change the world.

Harriet Tubman

Chapter 4

ENHANCE YOUR DREAMS WITH THE POWER OF INTENTION AND PROGRAMMING

The amazing journeys we embark on in our dreams, and the powerful guidance given to us in these realms and planes can be mesmerizing, but what if you don't remember your dreams? If your dreams fly by you as soon as you wake up, don't despair! It happens to even the most seasoned dream workers. In this chapter, we will take a look at some things you can do to better keep your dreams fresh in your mind as you wake up. The best remedy for deeper sleep and more dreams is to reduce the intake of mind-altering substances, which include both caffeine and alcohol, so try to experiment living without any caffeine and alcohol for a few weeks and see what happens to your dreams!

Whether or not you remember your dreams, you can rest assured that you dream —a lot! On average, we have about three to five dreams per night. So, even if you don't recall your dreams, are they still helpful? Yes! Dreams help you process unconscious reactions and emotions, so your unconscious side always benefits from your dreams. However, if you don't recall them in the morning, you miss out on the healthy awareness enhancing flow that would otherwise occur between your unconscious and conscious sides—not to mention all the beautiful messages, inspiration, and guidance that will pass you by! Without dream images clear in your mind and heart, it will be more difficult to identify guidance in your outer world as it happens, as you will not be able to experience the remarkable coincidences, or synchronistic events that occur when something in your daily life miraculously coincides with something you have just dreamt about!

When you are able to reflect upon, and truly work with, your dreams, the processing becomes conscious and stays with you. With enhanced awareness levels, you will not only feel better (because you have fewer unconscious emotional reactions), but you will also become more receptive to the guidance all around you.

So What Can You Do to Better Remember Your Dreams?

- Reduce your intake of any mind-altering substances, including caffeine and alcohol.

- Keep a dream journal by your bed and a pen nearby. When you wake up, write down anything you can remember, even if it is just a glimpse of a scene.

- Whatever image you can remember, keep it alive by reflecting upon it as you go about your day. If something happens in your daily life that reminds you of your dream, add a note in your dream journal.

- Go to bed with the intention to remember your dreams when you wake up in the morning! By having this intention as your drift off to sleep, you will actually program yourself to remember your dreams.

- You can also ask your dreams for guidance around a particular question or subject. You may also wish to write down this question in your journal.

- When you wake up in the morning, take some time to lie still in bed, while thinking about your dreams. I recommend keeping the journal nearby so that you can easily reach for it. Dreams often disappear once we start moving around and quickly fade as the minutes go by, so it is important to write down whatever you can recall as soon as possible.

Remember that dreams can seem very confusing at first! There is no need to filter and try to "make sense" of them as you recall them. Just write down whatever you can remember.

Once you have recorded your dream, you can start interpreting it (see chapter 3 for some useful tips):

- What types of emotions did you experience in the dream?
- What associations can you make with the symbols/events/people in the dream?
- How does the dream relate to your life right now?
- Did your dream answer your question...?

By practicing and being persistent, you can program and train yourself to better remember your dreams at night. Writing down your dreams in the morning, and asking your dreams for guidance at night, is a wonderful way of enhancing the flow!

Dream Incubation

You can ask your dreams for guidance about anything that's on your mind. Perhaps you need direction or help with your career, love life, finances, or health. Or maybe you want to develop your own intuitive abilities and be more open to premonitions and synchronicities coming your way. *Dream Incubation* is the term used to describe the process of asking your dreams for guidance. When you go to bed, develop a clear intention, and write down the question in your dream journal. There is a special power that develops from actually writing down a question. It is recommended that you only ask one question per night, as the messages can be very difficult to identify otherwise. Dreams are often confusing to begin with, so there is no need to complicate the process!

When you wake up in the morning, write down anything you can remember from the night, even if you don't think your dreams have answered your question. Once you take the time to process the dreams, you will start to see answers shining through! Keep the dream alive through the day, and be alert to any events in the outer world that remind you of a dream image. When you ask your dreams for guidance, stay open to even wider answers. The wisdom you are tapping into from the astral plane is infinite. You may get answers that go way beyond what you originally asked, if that is what your higher self knows will be in your best interest.

There is an ancient Chinese saying that so beautifully tells us...

"When the pupil is ready, the teacher will appear."

Your dreams provide you with the knowledge you need, when you are ready to receive it!

Crystal Clear Dreams

Crystals have been used all over the planet for thousands of years for their manifestation and healing abilities, and they are also beautiful dream enhancers. Life energy flows within and around you, and the unique energy vibrations from crystals have stimulating influences on your energy field. You can use crystals of a certain color and certain frequencies to aid dream recall and enhance your visits to dream realms.

Amethyst

Amethyst helps clear the aura and is a wonderful peaceful crystal that spreads harmony all around. If you feel anxious or worried that someone may be sending negative energy your way, it is a beautiful crystal to place under the pillow or next to you on the nightstand. The amethyst lovingly transforms negativity into positive energy and helps calm you down by releasing tension. It is also a good helper if you suffer from insomnia. In addition, it helps open the crown chakra, your higher awareness energy center above your head, and makes you more receptive to guidance coming your way.

Aventurine

The Aventurine crystal is a wonderful heart opener and helps you find trust and the inner knowing that all is working out. If you are experiencing feelings of anger during the day, it is a wonderful crystal to place on your heart chakra, the loving energy center around your heart area, as it helps clear and balance energies. Aventurine is also a powerful dream enhancer that not only stimulates dreaming, but also helps you release impatience. With trust in the outcome, you now have the power to make your dreams come true!

Moldavite

The Moldavite crystal was formed from rocks melting and merging with a giant meteorite that touched down in Eastern Europe over 15 million years ago. It is a high-vibration multidimensional crystal that helps develop your own clairvoyance, as well as wish-fulfillment abilities, by connecting you to higher planes and astral energies. It is particularly powerful when placed on the third eye chakra, the intuitive energy center between your eyebrows.

Tourmaline

This powerful crystal is a beautiful wisdom and love stone filled with inspiration, which also helps clear and purify energies all around. It comes in many colors. The blue tourmaline helps to activate your third-eye chakra—your clairvoyance and intuition center. So if you would like to dream more intuitive dreams, this is a great stone to place under your pillow. The green tourmaline inspires creativity and helps you dream of possible solutions to a problem. The pink tourmaline is a precious love stone that inspires you to trust in love. It helps you let go of negative feeling patterns in the heart and transforms these patterns into new, loving energies. The green and pink tourmalines are most helpful when placed on the heart.

Moonstone

The moonstone can help bring about lucidity in dreams. Lucid dreaming means you are fully aware that you are dreaming. Lucid dreams can be really exciting, and best of all, you will be able to recall the guidance even better when you wake up! The moonstone is also a beautiful emotional healing stone; it balances feminine and male energies and also calms down feelings of stress. Like amethyst, moonstone also helps you if you suffer from insomnia, so this is another great stone to place under your pillow if you have troubles falling asleep.

Everything that irritates us about others can lead us to an understanding of ourselves.

Carl Jung

Chapter 5

NIGTHMARES COME WITH URGENT MESSAGES!

Oh, the terror of nightmares! Cold chills are running down your spine, and the horrifying images from the dream can haunt you for hours. Your mind is going wild, and you may even wonder why you are being punished with something so awful and terrifying as a scary nightmare.

Everyone knows what it feels like to have a nightmare. Some people are even haunted by nightmares on a nightly basis. When a cold nightmare comes around, going to bed at night is often dreaded because of the fear that the dream will come back. It doesn't need to be that way! In contrast to the scary feeling they bring about, nightmares are actually here to help us heal.

The shock you experience in a nightmare is designed to capture your attention. There may be an unhealthy situation in your life that needs to change, or maybe there are unprocessed feelings and emotions blocking you up. These types of emotional blockages could turn life-threatening if they are not resolved. As you will see in this chapter, the healing path opens as soon as you acknowledge your dreams and start working with them. By facing your nightmares, you can actually transform their negative energy into something truly beautiful and loving.

Why Do We Have Nightmares?

Nightmares develop when we ignore an issue in our lives too long. Our "regular" nightly dreams help us become aware of any life situations to which we are not giving enough attention in our daily lives and help us solve dilemmas and find solutions to problems. If you choose to ignore the messages, or simply don't listen to your dream, it will come back, in stronger and scarier form, and eventually become so terrifying you no longer have a choice but not to ignore it. It is felt throughout your whole body, and you may even feel so terrified that you don't even want to go back to sleep, as you fear you may have it again. You are now fully aware of your dream! Your higher self has succeeded; the dream has made an impact on you, and you now have no choice but to listen.

If you still don't listen, the dream will come back to you. If it keeps haunting you in the same form, you are now having a recurring dream. Our dreams don't like being ignored! Sometimes you may even get different types of nightmares instead of recurring similar ones. In those situations, the dream is attempting different ways of getting the message through to you.

The best approach is therefore to work with all your dreams, because if you pay attention to your "regular' dreams, the risk of them developing into nightmares is significantly reduced (unless, of course, you are still not getting the message!). With some types of dreams and life situations, it is recommended to seek professional help. This applies in particular to nightmares that have developed from a real-life trauma, also known as PTSD: Post Traumatic Stress Disorder.

Real-Life Trauma Dreams

If you have experienced a real-life trauma and you are now having nightmares from the memory, it is important to work with them in the same manner as you would with "regular" nightmares. All types of nightmares are occurring to help you become more aware of what you need to work on in your daily life, and they bring about underlying feelings and emotional reactions that have not been properly processed and released.

If you are re-experiencing a terrifying event in your dreams that happened to you in real life, it is very important to process what happened. Some issues may require professional help. With some types of events and memories, the pain may never fully go away, and it is important to remember that the dream is not here to punish you and make it even worse for you! The nightmare is your friend. It is occurring to help you realize

that you still need to process the event further, and that there
are blocked emotions and unprocessed feelings within you.
Even though the pain may never disappear, once the
emotional connection to the feelings around the event has
been acknowledged, the pain will not carry as much weight as
it used to. Blocked emotions need to come out and be
experienced and felt. If this is not done, they will cause the
body to break down with various health issues.

So, a nightmare that developed from a real-life trauma is
here to help you process the event and release these blockages.
By paying attention to your nightmare and releasing the fear
around it, your pain will become more manageable with time,
and even though the pain from the trauma may still be there,
with the blocked emotions released, your body, mind, and soul
now have the power to heal again.

Nightmares from the Astral Plane

Every now and then a nightmare from the astral plane
sneaks through, and those can be particularly terrifying! There
are two types of astral nightmares:

1) The nightmare where an archetypal image, such as a
dragon or enormous snake, has been "borrowed" from the
astral plane to highlight something that is currently going on
in your life.

2) The nightmare where you have an actual visit from dark spirits, or take a trip to a terrifying place. If you are feeling unbalanced and emotionally weak, and also have high levels of substances in your body, including alcohol, you are more susceptible to being attacked by lower energies.

The second type of astral nightmares that involve "real" visits by darker beings is not common, but if you do have these types of dreams, the best remedy to keep these types of visits or voyages to dark faraway places from your peaceful realm is to surround yourself in white light before going to bed, and to stay away from recreational drugs. The combination of light and intention has the power to set you in the right vibrational frequency before drifting off to sleep. The other suggestions detailed below can be used with all types of nightmares, whether or not they were caused by a real-life trauma, or "dreamed up" by your higher self to highlight an issue that needs to be addressed, or even if they are caused by a dark astral visit!

How to Make Peace with Your Nightmare

You do not have to suffer from nightmares! Here are some steps you can take on your own to help highlight issues that need to be faced, release blocked emotions, and process what needs to be worked on. You have the power to heal, and the nightmares are here to help you!

The best way to deal with a nightmare is to figure out what issue the dream is trying to highlight, and then bring attention to the problem in your daily life. The nightmare is your friend, and it is here to help you with your pain!

Write Down the Nightmare

Even though you are feeling absolutely terrified when you

wake up from a nightmare, it is important to give the dream
the attention it is trying to bring you. Otherwise it will come
right back. It may still return that same night, but by writing
down the dream, you will have desensitized yourself to some
of the horror in it, and it will not have the same charge.

Work with Dream Associations

Look at all the symbols being portrayed in the dream. All
dream symbols were chosen for a reason. A symbol can be an
event, a dream figure, a location, sound, smell, etc. Write
down all associations you have for each of the symbols, and see
which associations "clicks" for you. What type of dream is it?
Nightmares are rarely intuitive in nature, as intuitive dreams
are typically not filled with emotions. Is the dream subjective,
objective, or astral? (See chapter 3.)

If the dream is objective in nature, and you are being
chased, think about what being chased means to you. Where
in your daily life have you experienced a similar feeling? What
are you running away from? Is it something you are avoiding
that needs to be faced? Perhaps there is someone you need to
confront? Most chasing dreams stop once we find a way to
deal with the issue we are afraid face in our daily life.

Reenter Your Nightmare and Ask for Guidance

This step is what Jung referred to as *Active Imagination*.[1]
You can enter a dream while awake and imagine you are
talking to the dream figures or the dream in general. Always
surround yourself in white light before entering a dream. Ask
the dream what it is trying to tell you and see what answers
you get. Write them down as well! Your underlying feelings
and fears are crying out to be acknowledged, and they will get
attention in this process. Once they are acknowledged, the
blockages are released, and you now have the room you need
to heal.

Create a New Ending

If the dream keeps coming back, decide on what you want
to do next time you're in it. Yes, it is possible to reprogram
yourself! This step will give you an immense sense of power
and control, and the effects from this mind-changing
reframing will reverberate throughout your daily life as well.
You are now creating the life you desire in your dreams, and
the changes will be felt on every level of your life. By
experiencing a resolution in your dream, you will feel more
secure in your daily life as well.

If you are experiencing a nightmare, remember it is here to help you *heal*. It is here as your friend, to help bring an urgent message. Something in your life needs to change! Or you may need to process unresolved emotional reactions. You will continue to suffer as long as you ignore your nightmares. By listening to your nightmare, you will receive the help you need to process blocked emotions, heal from past trauma, solve life situations you feel afraid of, and receive the guidance and inspiration you need to create the life you truly desire!

I do not know whether I was then a man dreaming I was a butterfly, or whether I am now a butterfly dreaming I am a man.

Zhuangzi

Chapter 6

GUIDANCE IS ALL AROUND YOU—LEARN HOW TO NOTICE SYNCHRONICITIES!

We all experience coincidences. In this chapter, we are not concerned with those daily little coincidences that pass us by as soon as they happen, such as two neighbor dogs running after the ball at the same time, or seeing your spouse in the morning after you dreamt about him or her that night. Instead, we're talking about the type of extraordinary coincidence that feels so surprising and remarkable that it has the power to shift your perceptions in the most powerful way imaginable.

If you were asked to reflect upon some peculiar coincidences in your own life, you could probably think of at least a few occurrences that were just too extraordinary to be considered everyday incidents. Perhaps something amazing happened that reminded you of a dream, or maybe you were thinking of a friend you had not seen in years, when he or she unexpectedly called you. Such events have the power to change our lives in a beautiful way, and even to fuel us with just the right amount of energy and trust to continue in a certain direction. An inner state, which could be a thought, a feeling, or a dream image, coincides with an outer event, and there is just no rational explanation for these types of occurrences. You just know that something meaningful, and something very important, is happening. You have experienced a synchronistic event!

The term synchronicity was originally coined by Carl Jung after he experienced some truly remarkable and meaningful coincidences himself.[1] In his definition of synchronicity, Jung was careful to differentiate synchronicity from a synchronous event with "meaning." A synchronous event can be described as anything that is happening at the same time. For example, school classes start at the same time in different schools, but no one sees anything significant in these "coincidences." In a synchronistic event however, the meaningful "coincidence" may well occur at the same time, but it is rather your own subjective reaction that is happening within you that brings the events together in a meaningful way.

Isn't it quite intriguing to think about how an image within you can suddenly show up in the outer world as well? Synchronistic events connect your inner and outer worlds! Even though someone next to you may very well see what is happening in this outer event, they cannot fully understand the significance, only you can, as you are the only one who knows what you were thinking about at the time. Hence when you are experiencing a synchronistic event, you can rest assured the guidance is for you only!

This connection, or the unity, between our inner and outer worlds was referred to by Jung as the *Unus Mundus*, "the potential world outside of time."[2] In the Unus Mundus, everything is interconnected, and there is no difference between the past, present, and future. Central to the Unus Mundus is the collective unconscious, the field shared by all living beings (see chapter 1). This concept forms a particularly important part of synchronicity, and can even be seen as the backbone of all synchronistic experiences, since this is the connected field we tap into when we dream. This powerful field is commonly referred to as the astral plane, and can also be seen as resembling the Eastern philosophy of an underlying Tao.

When we experience synchronicity, we begin to truly understand how everything around us really is interconnected, and how we get to tap into this power in our dream realms. Just imagine the possibilities you have every night when you go to sleep!

Our Teacher and Guide

When synchronistic experiences come our way, they are spontaneous and unexpected. In order to fully appreciate synchronicities, therefore, and to even notice them, awareness is the key! If we are not conscious about what we are thinking or feeling, how could we possibly see the link to something that is also happening around us?

Becoming aware of synchronistic events can have immense significance in your personal growth process. You can look at symbols in synchronistic events the same way you would when you interpret dreams, by asking yourself what they represent. In what way are you being guided? You can amplify the synchronistic event to see where this particular situation applies to your current life right now. A synchronistic event does not happen by chance, it has always come your way for a reason!

If you pay close attention to the symbols that showed up in your dreams before starting your day, the chances of experiencing a synchronistic event are much higher as you now are fully aware of your inner state.

Examples of Synchronicity

One of the best-known synchronicities experienced by Jung was preceded by a dream and beautifully shows the interconnectedness of our inner and outer worlds, and how this insight can help fuel a healing process. Jung was one day sitting in his office listening to one of his female clients sharing a dream she'd had the previous night about a golden scarab.[3] The same moment she talked about the scarab, there was a knock on the window, and when Jung turned around, he found to his astonishment that it was a beetle with a golden shine that was trying to get in. Jung's client was so surprised that she bounced up, and the event really helped her open herself up to the therapy process.

The dream of the scarab was an event in her inner psychic state, and this inner symbol was, in turn, mirrored by an outer event, in the form of a beetle. A beetle may possibly be the type of bug that looks most like a scarab, and it flew into the room just at a time when the therapy was progressing rather slowly and Jung felt the client was stuck. We can turn to mythology for further guidance when exploring what the scarab as a symbol may represent here. In his book *Synchronicity: An Acausal Connecting Principle*, Jung discusses how the scarab is used as a symbol for rebirth, for example in Egyptian mythology. So this synchronistic event can be seen as having helped the client become reborn, as it turned out to have such a significant and life-changing effect on the therapeutic process.[4]

The Number 137

Synchronicity events do not need to be of major size to have a significant impact. Sometimes the smallest events can provide the most astounding guidance. The following synchronistic event happened in my own life some years back and it beautifully inspired me to share my passion for dreams and synchronicity with more people.

A friend of mine I had just met three days earlier had given me a very interesting scientific journal to read about number archetypes and control theory. A central part of the study had to do with Wolfgang Pauli's fascination with the number 137. According to Pauli this number is highly special, and has been found to be the sum of all constants in nature.[5] Pauli was one of the true pioneers in quantum physics, and as a longtime student of Jung, I knew that Jung and Pauli had come to influence each other greatly in their respective fields, particularly with regard to synchronicity. As synchronicity had always fascinated me, I was now absolutely delighted to dive into this intriguing journal. A few minutes after reading the study, I decided to watch an old movie I had not seen in many years from the cable box movie gallery. I viewed the movie, and much to my surprise and astonishment, the number 1:37 flashed up on my screen just as it finished! In this modern era with DVDs and cable channels, the length of movies typically does not appear at the end, but since this was a purchased movie from the cable box, the movie length just popped up on the screen, in a large oversized font. I instantly felt very excited and inspired. I knew I was on the right track, and that this was a subject I needed to study closer and share with many people, immediately.

At the time, I was also part of the organizing committee for an upcoming regional conference for the International Association for the Study of Dreams. The next meeting happened to be held seven days later. Even though I had not initially planned on presenting a symposium at this conference, the synchronistic event I had experienced seven days earlier filled me with such inspiration and so much energy that I knew with all my heart that this was a subject I wanted to share with the world. In addition to the number 1:37 flashing up on the screen, we can find 137 in other places as well: I was given the journal on day one (1), which I read three days later (3), and seven days after that I felt guided to speak about this subject (7).

These beautifully connected events illustrate how even the smallest coincidences can serve as powerful guidance and help fuel us with the energy we need, and point us in the right direction, just when we need it!

All our dreams can come true, if we have the courage to pursue

them.

Walt Disney

Chapter 7

RECOGNIZE INTUITIVE AND PROPHETIC DREAMS

The most exciting dreams of all may be the ones that are mysteriously connected to events in the future, and dreams where we tap into the life of someone else! Some dreams can be highly revealing and sometimes so filled with premonitions they even stun us. You may, for example, dream about the name of someone you have never met before, and then you meet a person with just that name the very next day! Or you may dream about the new interiors of a friend's house, only to hear the next day that they have indeed redesigned their house exactly the way you saw it in your dream. Or perhaps you dream that your friend is feeling a certain way, just to hear the next day that it's true! When you tap into the feelings and thoughts of someone else, or receive direct information in some way, you are having a telepathic dream.

So What Do We Do with This Information?

Both in my therapeutic practice and in dream-guidance sessions, I encourage my clients to pay particular attention to events in their outer life that remind them of anything they have dreamt about. Whether it may be a literal telepathic dream, or a more symbolic synchronicity experience, any moments of guidance often occur at important transition points in our lives. As we saw in the earlier chapter, synchronistic events can help fuel us with the energy we need to continue in a certain direction, or they may help prepare us for a future event, so that we are better equipped when it actually happens.

Sometimes we dream about something that is happening, at the exact moment in time, in the outer world. For example, a person may be on holiday and dream about a fire in their home, and then receive a phone call at that exact point in time telling them that their house is, in fact, on fire. The fact that two events located far from each other in the physical realm can happen simultaneously in our inner and outer worlds make us realize that the concepts of both time and space may not be what we think they are. Jung, along with many other prominent researchers and scientists, proposed that neither space nor time consist of anything.[1] Rather, these are concepts we have constructed in order to make sense of our experiences. Synchronistic and telepathic phenomena really show how inner and outer events can occur simultaneously. Simultaneous or not simultaneous, the events in synchronistic and telepathic events are so deeply connected, they are not limited by time and space![3]

How Do We Know When We Receive Guidance in Dreams?

Clients often ask me about messages in dreams. How do we know when we are receiving true guidance, when we are having a telepathic dream, and which types of dreams are more oriented toward helping us process our feelings and emotions? How do we know when we're receiving a premonition, so we can take action?

I have been working with dreams for a long time, and because I have a background as both a therapist and an intuitive, I really like these questions. All types of dreams are equally important. Just because you may not be receiving messages to solve the mystery of the universe in a dream, it doesn't mean you are not growing! Every single dream you have helps you in one form or the other. Dreams may not always offer you premonitions, but many dreams can help you work through unconscious feelings and reactions, and the process in itself helps remove the emotional blockages that are weighing you down. Dreams also help enhance your awareness, and as you clear your own energy from emotional blockages, you become more receptive to receiving guidance, not only in your dreams, but also in your daily life.

So how can you know when you are processing emotional feelings, and when you are having an intuitive dream? The answer is easier if you are aware enough to reflect upon how you're feeling! If you're feeling *emotionally charged* and really involved in a dream, the chances are higher that the dream is helping you process an emotional feeling or highlight an issue in your life that you may be unaware of.

On the other hand, if you're experiencing something in a dream without any significant feelings attached to it, and you may even feel like you're watching a movie, then you may indeed be receiving intuitive guidance or experiencing a telepathic dream. Also, intuitive dreams typically are more "sequential" and logical in nature, with a proper story line developing, whereas emotional dreams tend to be more incoherent.

In telepathic dreams, we generally tap into the feelings or life issues of someone else instead of processing our own emotions and feelings, and as a general rule of thumb, we tend to feel more like we're "a fly on the wall" in those types of dreams. We are just making a quick visit, and if we are interacting with any dream characters, the discussion can be surprising in nature, but it doesn't usually stir up too much of an emotional reaction. Rather than feeling upset, we are taking in the information, treasuring every moment.

With regard to "taking action" after having had an intuitive dream, it needs to be noted that there is just not much we can do with some types of premonitions. We may have received an image about an upcoming event in a dream, but we often don't have enough information to make sense of it, or even to know when or where it will happen. Many people dreamt about the World Trade Centre attack in September 2011 during the nights and even weeks preceding the tragic event. However, even though many of the dreams involved fire, airplanes, and columns, they did not contain enough information to say where the tragedy would take place, and who would be involved.

Sometimes intuitive dreams come to us to help us prepare for events, and to make it easier to handle them as they happen. At other times, they help us pay extra attention to such events, as there may be important value in them. There may be a major significance and link to a particular event, also in your own personal life. See what is happening in your life right now, and how the premonition you had may also relate to your own life circumstances. Likewise, if you are having a telepathic dream about a friend's current life circumstances, ask yourself why this information has been revealed to you as this particular point in time. How do you benefit from receiving this knowledge right now?

Intuition Enhancement

The best way of enhancing your intuition is to pay close attention to your dreams every morning and to practice higher awareness on an everyday basis. By keeping your dream images alive throughout the day, you become more receptive to the symbols, messages, and parallel events that are happening in your daily life.

You can also boost your own intuition by asking yourself questions at night before you go to sleep. Begin with easier questions, such as what song you will hear playing on the radio the next day, or who will call you first thing in the morning. With time, you can advance your questions by wishing to receive guidance about certain situations, or help with major life decisions. Pay close attention to your dreams as you wake up, and look for any clues that may have been revealed to you. By processing each dream in detail (see chapter 3), the messages will start shining through, even if, at first, you may not think the dream has provided you with any guidance.

Remember, guidance comes your way when you are ready to receive it. By continuously working with your dreams, you keep enhancing your awareness levels and become even more receptive to the beautiful messages that are there for you. It is truly a win-win situation!

The interpretation of dreams is the royal road to a knowledge of the unconscious activities of the mind.

Sigmund Freud

Chapter 8

QUESTIONS TO ASK WHEN INTERPRETING DREAMS

The dream interpretation examples in this chapter have been chosen to help you move in the right direction as you explore your own dreams to better understand their meanings. Even though your dreams are indeed uniquely personal to you in many ways, there are some common dream themes that we all encounter from time to time, and it is some of those "popular types of dreams" that are highlighted here, along with some good sample questions you can ask your dreams as you unveil their real message!

In contrast to the more generic guides you typically find in popular dream dictionaries, the dream interpretation approach I have developed is more intuitive in nature in that it emphasizes the importance of your *feelings* in the dream, and also assists you in establishing the context by encouraging you to ask specific *questions* about the dream. Your own intuition will ultimately be the best guide as you decode the different symbols. The context, or setting, such as dreaming of a dolphin in a bathtub, may have very different meanings to you than it would for someone else, depending not only on what you felt and experienced in the dream, but also on your background and the personal associations you have with both dolphins and bathtubs. A dream dictionary may, for example, tell you that a dolphin symbolizes happiness and joy, and that a bathtub represents rejuvenation or "cleansing," but it will most likely fail to ask you what you personally associate with dolphins or bathtubs. It may also ignore the fact that a bathtub in this situation could also be viewed as "restricting." Why is the dolphin in such a small space? Perhaps you have a unique memory of a dolphin, or have always been intrigued by dolphins for some specific reason. Did something of significance ever happen to you in a bathtub? What does a dolphin mean to you? At the end of the day, you are the only one who will ever know for sure what the dream really meant, and it is your own intuition that will help guide you more than anything else!

Animal Kingdom

Animals are symbolic characters, and just like people, they appear in our dreams for a very specific reason. Animal dreams are often very spiritual in nature, and many native tribes believe that animals in our dreams empower us with the qualities of their spirit, and they are also viewed as our guardians.

Sometimes animals are brought into your dream to help highlight parts of yourself in one form or the other. Animals also appear in intuitive and astral dreams as special messengers of important information. If you are dreaming of a pet who has passed over, it could be an astral visit!

Insights from the Animal Kingdom

What comes to mind when you think about the type of animal in your dream? *Eagles, dolphins, and elephants* are all very spiritual animals, and often show up in astral dreams with specific messages and insights for us. What comes to mind when you think of elephants? For many people, elephants symbolize wealth and abundance, along with spiritual insights. Depending on your own personal history and background, the associations you make with each animal in your dream will be helpful clues in the dream interpretation process.

A fascinating dream symbol is the *snake*. Snakes represent so many things, naturally they can be highly dangerous and poisonous, but they also bring wisdom and new beginnings. If you are dreaming of a snake, on a subjective level it could very well indicate that you have some snake-like qualities within you—perhaps you are more venomous to people around you than you think, but the snake may also have appeared to help you find your own inner wisdom. Your feelings in the dream will help guide you to see what's really going on.

On a more objective level, the dream could highlight that you feel someone in your surrounding is attacking you, and the dream could help you process the situation. Symbolic snakes are popular visitors from the astral plane and could enter your dream as an archetypal force to highlight something that is going on in your life, or to bring a unique message to you.

Astral dreams can also occur in dream states where we are half sleeping and half awake, and dream figures from the animal kingdom sometimes make an appearance in this realm. If you "wake up" at night and see a beautiful unicorn standing next to you, listen to your heart. Messages from the animal kingdom are conveyed through feelings. A miraculous visit filled with love and light will of course make you feel better than a dark visit by spiders and bugs. If you are attracting lower energy visitors, go back to chapter 5 and learn how to surround yourself with white light before going to bed.

Chasing Dreams

Many of us have been chased by a frightening being in our dream at some point. On a subjective level, a chasing dream could appear to help you see that you may be running away from something that is going on within you. Taking a more objective approach, you could be trying to get away from someone around you, or from a specific situation in your daily life. Nightmares of being chased are very common, and help showcase how we either live in denial, or don't face our fears in daily life.

Insights from Being Chased

Ask yourself what it is you may be afraid of facing. What are you running away from? Is there a side to yourself you may not see, or perhaps feel uncomfortable about? Or are you trying to escape from a situation or avoiding someone in your life? Think about what it is you fear in life. By asking yourself these questions, you build up higher awareness about what is really going on in your life, and you will find the strength to deal with your situation.

Chasing dreams will keep haunting you until you develop higher awareness about yourself, and until you are able to work through and face what you are scared of. When you are being chased it is time to take a big leap into the tiger's mouth and face your fears!

Driving Dreams

How you drive your car or any other type of vehicle in a dream can help you see what is really happening in your life right now. How is your journey? Are you traveling through life smoothly, or are you going backward and spinning out of control in all directions?

Insights from Driving Dreams

Can you see the road in front of you, or is it all dark? Are the breaks functioning? If you're about to crash or actually do crash in the dream, it could be a warning sign that this is the direction in which your life is moving if you don't do anything to change things around. It could of course also be a reflection that something has already gone wrong in your life. What can you do to rectify the situation? Remember, when one door closes another door opens!

If you're driving up a hill but don't have enough power to continue, but instead start rolling backward, it is a good indication that this is also how you feel in your life right now. You're almost there, but you can't quite make it. Think about what happened the day prior to the dream, take up the context, and see how it relates to your current life circumstances. You are receiving guidance every night!

Dying in Dreams

Death in dreams rarely indicates that you or someone else is actually dying. If someone is really about to die in real life, most guidance in dreams tends to be more symbolic. For instance, instead of dreaming about a relative's actual death, you may dream that they are standing next to you with a packed suitcase, symbolizing that they are "going away." A dream of an actual impending death often has more life-changing themes, such as moving to a new place, or embarking on a long journey. So if you dream that you are dying, it most likely does not foretell that you are. However, it could be a good indication that it is time for you to thoroughly examine what is going on in your life. A situation as you know it may now have ended.

Insights about Dying in Dreams

If you died in the dream, ask yourself in what way a situation in your life has ended right now. Remember, endings are followed by new beginnings, and new doors will open! Now may be a good time for you to pause and reflect. By focusing inward you will find your true path.

Emotions in Dreams

Emotions in dreams are highly indicative of how you are really feeling, and such dreams can be worth their weight in gold, especially in times of denial and when you are lying to yourself. As most dreams are highly subjective and try to highlight things about you, the way other people feel in your dream is often a reflection of your own inner emotional state.

Insights from Emotions in Dreams

If there are *sad* people around you, this could be a sign that it is actually you who are feeling sad. Take the time to heal and remember that forgiveness is the most powerful healer. If your dream is filled with *angry* people, this could be a reflection of your own unprocessed or unresolved anger. It may be time for you to let go of past disappointments. Of course, the dream could also be objective and help you understand a relationship better by bringing about all the feelings and emotions involved.

Fairies in Dreams

Fairies sometimes visit us in dream realms and give us a sparkling touch of magic and belief! They often appear in difficult times, just as we need love and hope the most. Like visitors from the animal kingdom, fairy encounters often happen in astral dreams when we are half awake and half asleep. These types of dreams are so miraculous and special that they may even stay with us forever after.

Insights from Fairies in Dreams

What is happening in your life right now? What were you thinking about before going to sleep? There are many fascinating stories about people who have had visits from fairies in times of despair and distress, and how they beautifully woke up with a magical spark of excitement, and a wonderful sense of belief in miracles all around! These types of dreams can feel amazingly real, and you may also be taken on an "actual voyage" to the land of the fairies, or receive a little surprise visit from a fairy in your own home.

Falling Dreams

When you're falling in a dream, whether in a freefall or in an elevator that is heading down, this is a good indication it's time to reevaluate your life situation. Whereas going up in life is considered positive, falling downward is generally not an encouraging sign. These types of dreams are often warning signals, so it is important to pay close attention to what is happening.

Insights from Falling Dreams

Ask yourself where in your life you may feel like something is not going the way you planned. The solution you're seeking may be right in front of you. Remember there is a positive in each situation, and it is important not to focus too much on the negative. What can you do to fix it? Can you redirect what is happening somehow? If it is not possible to physically do something about the situation, remember you can always change your attitude, inviting more positive thoughts into your life. By processing what's happening, you clear energetic blockages and now have the space to attract more positive thoughts.

Flying Dreams

Whether you're flying by yourself or in an airplane, flying in a dream brings feelings of ultimate freedom, happiness, and excitement, and from a spiritual perspective, many people believe flying in a dream is actually an astral projection, where our soul leaves our body to explore other realms!

Insights from Flying Dreams

Whether you are flying on your own, or in an airplane, you are reaching new heights, and this may also be how you feel in daily life. Now is a great time to really stretch your wings and fly! You may have been underestimating your own abilities, and the dream has appeared to help you develop more belief in yourself.

If you're afraid of *crashing*, or actually do crash, this could indicate that your life is out of control in some way. Where may this be applicable? Any type of crash dream is often a warning sign that you need to change what you are currently doing, so pay close attention to such dreams!

Sometimes we spread our wings so high that we reach

new realms altogether. High above the clouds you may find a
sacred land, or golden temple filled with unique wisdom, just
for you, just when you need it the most. These types of
miraculous dreams are astral in nature, and the insights gained
from such journeys can be life changing.

Hair Loss Dreams

Losing your hair in a dream can be very distressing. How
you feel in the dream often reveals the true story, so think
about what effect the hair loss or haircut in the dream had on
you. Did you feel happy and excited about the change or
absolutely devastated? Hair could be associated with
personality, beauty, self-confidence, power, and youth. Think
about what is going on in your life right now, and how these
events are affecting you.

Insights from Hair Loss Dreams

If you're a woman and dream of losing your hair, it may be
an indication that you're not feeling very feminine at the
moment. Perhaps your partner has lost sexual interest. If
you're a man and your hair falls off, or is cut off too short,
think about what may be causing you to feel this way. Maybe
you lost out on a project at work, or perhaps a younger
colleague got the promotion you've been working so hard for.

If you dream that your *scalp is falling off* as well, the changes you're currently experiencing may now be affecting you to the point that you are really hurting. The notion that your scalp is tearing puts an extra spin on such dreams. Whatever personal associations you have with your hair, they all need your "scalp" to flourish and grow. If the scalp is not there, it means all the qualities you associate with your hair will not be able to grow back until you heal the scalp. These types of dreams could be strong warning dreams, urging you to take precautions and rectify the situation.

House Dreams

A house in a dream is often a representation of you, it is your own sacred temple! Do you feel safe in the house? Is it old or new, filled with inspiration or sadness? Remember any symbols in the dream, such as open or closed doors, floors, and also pay attention to any new rooms that you may find.

Insights from House Dreams

If you feel safe, and the house is *fresh and bright,* it could signify that you feel calm and happy in your life right now, whereas dreaming of a *little shed* that is falling apart in an earthquake may indicate that you are not grounded enough and may need to place more focus in your daily life on creating more security for yourself.

Doors in a dream often indicate that you have some decisions to make. If the doors are closed, it may not be quite your time yet. Think about where this may currently apply in your life. If the doors are open, the dream may show you it is time to move ahead now; you can move forward! There are no blockages and the door is open! Open doors could also be an intuitive sign that great new opportunities are coming your way, or are perhaps already present around you.

Dark houses, as well as dark dreams in general, often show lack of awareness. You can enhance your awareness by paying more attention to your dreams and dedicating yourself to a daily meditation practice.

When you stumble upon *new rooms* in a dream house, or even new stores in a shopping mall, you could be finding something new about yourself. Perhaps you are not aware of your full potential and everything you are capable of. It is important to ask yourself what type of room you have found.

A *basement* could be a representation of your unconscious. Pay close attention to what is happening down there! You can learn a lot about yourself.

A *higher floor* on the other hand often shows your higher self, and your higher potential. Perhaps you are reaching new insights.

A *sink, bathtub or shower* often appears in our dreams when we have done something we feel guilty or uncomfortable about, or when we feel ready to "cleanse" ourselves.

Lost in Dreams

When you dream that you are lost, chances are that this is also how you feel in waking life. You may be feeling confused, or maybe even meaningless inside, as though you don't know the way forward. You may have been distracted from your true path, or lost connection with family and friends, and the dream has appeared to help you find your way again.

Insights from Being Lost

If you *can't find your way*, or don't know where you are, think about where in your life you feel lost right now. By implementing a daily meditation practice you can enhance your awareness, and help find inner peace and a sense of purpose and direction.

If there is *fog* in your dream, ask yourself what it is you may not want to see in your waking life. As with all dreams, your personal background, life situation, and memories will ultimately guide you as you find the true message in a dream.

Lovemaking Dreams

Lovemaking dreams can be so beautiful and feel amazingly real. You may not always know the person you're making love with in your dream, but as we have touched upon earlier, when we dream about other people, what our dream is really trying to do on a subjective level is to show us different aspects of ourselves, and in sex dreams the emphasis is often on our feminine and masculine aspects. As mentioned earlier in this book, in the Jungian school of psychology, our feminine and masculine qualities are referred to as anima and animus. The feminine side within a man is his anima, and the masculine side of a woman is her animus.[1] As long as our anima and animus are unconscious we are not utilizing our full abilities, and we may even feel "possessed" or surprised by our unknown reactions! Lovemaking dreams are a great way of bringing these qualities into consciousness.

Insights from Lovemaking Dreams

Do you feel in balance? If you're dreaming of making love to *someone you know*, remember that the person in your dream has been chosen for a very specific reason! What comes to mind when you think about your dream lover? What do you like about him or her? On a subjective level, a lovemaking dream may be trying to tell you that you would benefit from taking on some of the qualities of that particular person. From an objective perspective, it could also be a sign that it would be good for you to work with them closer—perhaps there is a project developing on the horizon? If you are making love to an ex-partner, you may now be ready to move "beyond the hurt." Perhaps you feel ready to forgive and forget and move on with your life. It could also signify that you still love them, and that you will always have a beautiful connection.

If you don't know the partner in your dream, on a subjective level, the partner could indeed be an aspect of yourself. Reflect upon how your lover acted, and if there are any personality characteristics that may also be present within you. If you're a woman making love to a man, what stands out about him? He likely represents your animus, your masculine qualities. Do you see yourself in him? Could you benefit from expressing yourself more like the man in your dream? From a more objective perspective, the dream could help you feel truly loved. Treasure such dreams and keep them alive as you go about your day! When you feel happy and resonate on a higher frequency, and feel as if what you wish for has already happened, that's when you begin to attract good things all around!

As with all dreams, lovemaking dreams could also be intuitive guidance dreams, in which case your dream lover may be waiting for you around the corner!

Mandala Dreams

A mandala is a beautiful round symbol that often contains geometrical shapes. *Mandala* is a Sanskrit word for "circle." Mandalas can sometimes appear spontaneously in our dreams or during meditations. A mandala is a very powerful dream symbol and shows up to both guide and heal you! Dreams of mandalas often come about when we are in the process of finding our true path. The circular image symbolizes healing and integration. The mandala can be seen as a beautiful circular force integrating all aspects of yourself.

Insights from Mandala Dreams

When a mandala appears, whether in a dream or during a meditation, it is a sign you are finding your real calling. How can you best stay on your true path? What have you done lately that symbolizes healing and integration? If you notice yourself experiencing more inner peace from meditation and dream work, keep up the good work!

Naked Dreams

Most people have found themselves naked in a dream at some point in their lives. These types of dreams are mainly subjective, and come about to highlight how we feel about ourselves. Some naked dreams can be very embarrassing, whereas others make us feel like we're giving away too much of ourselves, or that people can see right through us.

Insights from Being Naked in Dreams

If you are *naked* in a dream, you may recently have revealed something embarrassing, or felt exposed somehow and did not enjoy it—maybe you felt unprepared and afraid everyone saw it. It could also be a sign that you are guilty about something in your life right now. Perhaps something you have said or done? Maybe you have talked too much about yourself or someone else?

If you feel *naked and happy,* it would probably do you good if you showed more of yourself, perhaps you would benefit from being more honest and show people who you really are. As always, when you work with your dreams, think about how you felt in the dream, and the answer will come to you.

Pregnancy / Baby

Dreaming of a new life growing within you could be a sacred message that you really are pregnant, or a premonition that you will be blessed with a baby soon! In other instances, these types of dreams reflect the potential for growth in your life. A new birth could be about to happen, perhaps within you.

Insights from Pregnancy / Baby Dreams

The baby developing inside you could represent some

beautiful changes happening within you. The baby you are about to give birth to, or have just given birth to, may indeed be a new you. Are you perhaps about to transform your life in some way? Think about what projects you have going on that may be blossoming right now? If you can't think of any, this may be a very good time to develop something. Are there perhaps some new ideas cooking on the stove? Look around you and see what is happening and use the guidance from the dream as you make your decisions to move forward or continue in a new direction.

School and Exams

Being back in school is a popular dream, and this type of dream is often highly subjective in nature, as it shows what is currently going on within you. When you dream that you're back in school, it is a good indication that you're not feeling prepared for something, and it's time to brush up your knowledge a bit.

Insights from School and Exam Dreams

If you suddenly find yourself taking an *exam* you haven't studied for you're probably feeling overwhelmed or simply unprepared in daily life. You may have an important meeting coming up that you don't feel ready for. Take a good look at your situation and see what you can do to acquire the knowledge you need to feel better equipped and more confident that you are indeed good enough and know enough!

Stuck or Powerless in Dreams

Being stuck or feeling powerless in a dream often reflects that you wish your life were different in some way, but you feel unable to do something about it. You may be struggling with a decision, or feel the need to move on. Trust your own intuition and move forward!

Insights from Being Stuck or Powerless in Dreams

Where do you feel stuck right now? Around what issues do you have conflicting emotions? What can you do to free yourself and get your power back? Can you perhaps develop a new attitude? Your own inward search for answers will reward you. Think about what aspects of your life you can change.

The Serenity prayer beautifully tells us:

"God grant me the serenity to accept the things I cannot change; courage to change the things I can; and wisdom to know the difference."

Train Dreams

You may be about to embark on an important journey in your life. Train dreams are often very symbolical. As opposed to many other types of traveling dreams, trains are different in that they follow a set schedule, and even have a specific destination.

Insights from Train Dreams

If you are running toward a train, you may feel like you're about to miss out on an important opportunity in your waking life. If you jump on the train too fast, without bringing your luggage, it may indicate that you are rushing in life and will end up wasting time because you now have to go back again and get what you forgot. Pay close attention to your feelings in the dream.

Unfaithful Dreams

If you dream that your partner is having an affair, take a deep breath. They may not be. If you are feeling highly emotionally charged in the dream, it will do you better if you give them the benefit of the doubt. In those instances, it is most likely an objective emotional processing dream, which is designed to help you work through a certain life situation or emotion. On a subjective level, it could even be you who are being unfaithful to yourself.

Insights from Unfaithful Dreams

If you have no reason to suspect that you are being wronged, think about what may be causing you to feel that your partner is not being honest with you. From a subjective perspective, it could be you who are not being honest with yourself. Perhaps there is something you need to learn about yourself, that is being shown to you through the dream actions of your partner. You may be feeling empty inside, and seek more meaning and rewards. You may even be yearning to leave some aspects of your life behind, and it is now time to fill any voids in your life in healthy ways.

On the other hand, if you dreamt about the affair without feeling upset, and perhaps even felt like you were watching a movie without having any emotional reaction, it could indeed indicate that you are being guided to see what is really going on around you.

Water Dreams

Water in dreams is sometimes a reflection of the deep unconscious part of you, and it can also represent your emotions. If the water is calm and clear, this is likely also how you feel in your daily life—you feel happy and have clarity. In contrast, if the water is dark, you may be experiencing sadness and confusion.

Insights from Water Dreams

What is the color of the water? Is it dark or light? Are the waves high, and are they crashing over you? Maybe you are experiencing a very difficult situation in life, and the dream is here to bring more awareness of your situation.

Sitting on the beach, gazing out over a beautiful pink ocean with magical fairy sparks allover will naturally feel very different from being lost at sea! Your feelings in the dream will help serve as beautiful road signs as you find the true answers you are looking for.

In the state of love, no matter what you do, it's going to be

good.

Paramahansa Yogananda

Chapter 9

INVITE MIRACLES INTO YOUR LIFE USING THE GUIDANCE FROM YOUR DREAMS!

Dreams are truly magical in so many ways. In this book so far, we have seen how we are not only receiving beautiful guidance and special messages while sleeping, but also how the guidance is all around us also in our waking lives. The interconnectedness between our inner and outer worlds is truly astonishing. There is so much more going on both within and around us than first meets the eyes, and our dream world really shows how life is not always what it seems. For example, if time and space were set in stone, how could we possibly have a dream about a person we haven't seen in years and then receive an important phone call from them the next day? Or how could we dream about something that is happening at that very moment, somewhere far away in another part of the world? Synchronistic experiences and prophetic dreams help show us that our inner and outer worlds are strongly connected. When we are being guided, we tap into something much larger than ourselves, and concepts such as time and space just seem to disappear!

You can enhance your intuition every day, just by paying attention to your dreams in the morning. By keeping your dream energies alive throughout the day, you become even more open to related messages and symbols around you. Your dream images may not always be followed by exact parallel images in the outer world. Rather, *symbolic versions of a dream image* are more likely to show up in your external life. You may see something on a TV news channel, a book in a bookstore, or a specific person that reminds you of something from your dream. Pay particular attention to those moments. You are being guided for a reason! Often the meaning is not clear in the dream itself, and it is not revealed until later. Keeping careful track of your dreams in a dedicated dream journal will make it much easier for you to spot these moments as they happen. With dream work and higher awareness, you receive the beautiful guidance and energy that you need to take you to the next place, and you now open the way for true miracles to come through.

All about Polarity!

Have you ever thought about how life can be seen as being built on opposites? Think about it! We are either on the lower or higher end of any spectrum, or somewhere in between. In the ancient text *The Kybalion*, which outlines basic hermetic teachings, the legendary sage Hermes Trismegistus discusses that life is all about polarities and opposites.[1]

The Principle of Polarity is discussed in the Fourth
Hermetic Principle:

"Everything is Dual; everything has poles; everything has its pair
of opposites; like and unlike are the same; opposites are
identical in nature, but different in degree; extremes meet; all
truths are but half-truths; all paradoxes may be reconciled."

If we look at life from a perspective of polarities,
everything can indeed be seen as having two sides. There is
just more or less of something, with manifold degrees between
the two extremes. You can consciously choose to vibrate at
either end of the spectrum. But if you are weighed down with
blockages and negative energy patterns, it will be hard to
remain on the higher end. Here, again, we see the true beauty
of working with our dreams and clearing out negative
influences, to ensure we clear the space for positive
affirmations and manifestations! Without blockages in the
way, you are free to move around the spectrum of polarities as
you wish, and you are now in a much better place. You are
consciously creating, rather than reacting to live events and
being pushed up and down the pole.

Conflict Resolution

How can we stay open to miracles and helpful guidance if
we are constantly overwhelmed by conflicts? Trust, and let go!
When we trust in a good outcome, the law of opposites helps
bring about a solution that matches our belief somewhere
along the spectrum of polarities. The best part of letting go is
that, by doing so, our conscious self (which is our ego with
limited awareness) is no longer the key player in the outcome,
but rather our higher self (which has access to all aspects of
ourselves, as well as the vast field shared by us all—the
collective unconscious) now takes over and creates a new
solution for us. The new and powerful answer is often
presented to us in a dream or through a symbolic meaningful
coincidence in our outer world, as a synchronicity. So, next
time you are in doubt about something, or have to make a
difficult decision, trust in a good outcome and let it be for a
while. The best way to create a miraculous solution is to sleep
on it, and let your higher self guide the way!

By paying more attention to your dreams, you begin
tapping into the magnificent dream field on a higher
vibrational level, and this is how the flow really opens up for
beautiful miracles in your life. Dream analysis helps you let go
of negative energy and self-destructive thought patterns and
helps you create much more space for positive thoughts when

you remove those negative blockages.

You now have more room to create, affirm, and manifest the life you really desire, and you also become more open to miracles as they come your way. Every time you pay attention to a dream, you develop higher awareness, which will help you understand your dreams even better.

Trust is the key to manifesting a new direction in life, or affirming something beautiful to happen. The well-known spiritual text *A Course in Miracles*[2] states:

"Those who trust in the outcome can afford to wait, and wait without anxiety."

The truth is that you already have the power within you to create the life you truly desire. More important than anything is the ability to really trust and let go of negative anxiety. Assume the feeling that what you wish for has already happened, and you're now not only where you need to be, but also where you want to be. Feel as though what you wish for has already happened and is now true. Dreams help us miraculously in the affirmation process by removing negative blockages, and even more so by making us receptive to guidance and opening room for more positive thought forms to take place.

Wish-Fulfillment Dreams Prepare for Miracles

In addition to being filled with beautiful guidance and uniquely specific messages, dreams also help prepare you for new events coming your way. If you are having a wish-fulfillment dream, make the most of that dream as you wake up! Remember and experience with your whole body, mind, and soul what it felt like to have that wish come true in your dream, and create an affirmation that resonates with this feeling. Let's say you dreamt of moving into your dream house. As you wake up in the morning, resume that feeling all over and let your happiness reverberate everywhere around and inside you. Write down a positive affirmation, such as:

I have found my dream home, and I resonate with gratitude and love.

You can use the messages from your dreams to create powerful and positive affirmations for your life. Best of all, by paying more attention to the guidance you receive, your dreams will become even more unique and powerful and will really help you understand the power of holding your thoughts on a positive frequency.

One night I had a beautiful dream, in which I could change whatever I touched into whatever I wished for. In my dream, I even created a whole new street and changed the color of the sky!

This is a great example of a wish-fulfillment dream, and the creative power we have within us. Whenever you have a positive wish dream, I recommend tapping into the feeling of that dream as you prepare for beautiful new events in your life. By taking on the feeling that what you wish for has already happened, you enter a much higher vibrational state, and you are now more receptive to guidance and miracles as they come your way.

Here are some examples of miraculous dream affirmations, all inspired from the magnificent dream realms:

Anything I see and experience, I can change; I see what I believe.

*

I am flying safely in higher dimensions, and I am floating in the air like a ship on water.

*

In my dreams, I tap into love wisdom and I receive guidance.

*

I choose positive thoughts.

*

The Wise Old Man has invited me to higher realms; I am here
now.

*

I create and direct my own life.

*

I am vibrating on higher frequencies.

*

I am abundant in every aspect of my life, and I happily share
my gifts.

*

Remember our earlier point about time and space?
Whenever in doubt about something in your life, there is
nothing more powerful than to remind yourself that
everything is really not what it seems. You have the wonderful
ability to shape many events around you, and what better
place to receive the guidance you need to do so than from your
own dreams? Make use of all the beautiful messages coming
your way, and start creating the life you really desire.

Dreams are inspirational in so many ways, and I hope this book has inspired you to go a bit deeper as you embark on your inner journey and create your own dream life. As you ask your dreams for guidance, remember that you may sometimes receive answers that go well beyond your original question! Because your higher self is connected to the collective unconscious, dreams have the power of bringing about pretty much anything that has ever been of significance in the life of humanity.

When you are ready to receive a message, guidance, or premonition, you will! So get ready to tap into an infinite level of wisdom tonight, and let your dreams lead the way...

Sweet Dreams!

Anna-Karin

Dream Big

Hope for the Best

Expect a Miracle!

Biographical Notes

Introduction

1 Jung, C.G. (1974). *Dreams*. Princeton, NJ: Princeton
   University Press

2 Moss, R. (2005). *Dreamways of the Iroquois: Honoring the
   Secret Wishes of the Soul*. Rochester, Vermont: Destiny
   Books.

3 Von Franz, M-L. (1985). *Dreams: A Study of the Dreams of
   Jung, Descartes, Socrates, and Other Historical Figures*.
   Boston, MA: Shambhala Publications, Inc.

Chapter 1

1 Weitz, L. (1976). Jung's and Freud's Contributions to Dream
   Interpretation: A Comparison. *American Journal of
   Psychotherapy*, 30(2), 289. Retrieved from:
   http://search.ebscohost.com/login.aspx?direct=true&d
   b=pbh&AN=5352989&site=ehost-live

2 Jung C.G (1959). *The Archetypes and the Collective
   Unconscious*. New York, N.Y: Princeton University
   Press.

3 Ibid.

4 Jung C.G. (1974). *Dreams.* Princeton, NJ: Princeton University Press

5 Jung C.G. (1959). *The Archetypes and the Collective Unconscious.* New York, N.Y: Princeton University Press

6 Ibid.

7 Ibid.

8 Jung C.G. (1966). *The Practice of Psychotherapy: Essays on the Psychology of the Transference and Other Subjects.* New York, N.Y: Princeton University Press.

9 Ibid.

10. Jung, C.G. (1963). *Memories, Dreams, Reflections.* New York, NY: Random House

Chapter 2

1 Jung C.G. (1966). *The Practice of Psychotherapy.* New York, N.Y: Princeton University Press.

2 Ibid.

3 Jung C.G (1959). *The Archetypes and the Collective Unconscious.* New York, N.Y: Princeton University Press

Chapter 3

1 Jung C.G. (1974). *Dreams.* Princeton, NJ: Princeton
    University Press

Chapter 5

1 Johnson, R.A. (1986). *Inner Work: Using Dreams and Active
    Imagination for Personal Growth.* New York, NY.
    Harper Collins

Chapter 6

1 Jung, C.G. (1960). *Synchronicity: An Acausal Connecting
    Principle.* New York: NJ: Bollingen Foundation.

2 Jung, C.G. (1963). *Memories, Dreams, Reflections.* New York,
    NY: Random House.

3 Jung, C.G. (1960). *Synchronicity: An Acausal Connecting

Principle.* New York: NJ: Bollingen Foundation.

4 Ibid.

5 Varlaki, P. (2008). Number Archetypes and "Background"
    Control Theory Concerning the Fine Structure
    Constant. *Acta Polytechnica Hungarica.* 5 (2).

Chapter 7

1 Jung, C.G. (1960). *Synchronicity: An Acausal Connecting Principle*. New York: NJ: Bollingen Foundation.

Chapter 8

1. Jung C.G (1959). *The Archetypes and the Collective Unconscious.* New York, N.Y: Princeton University Press

Chapter 9

1 Three Initiates (2008). *The Kybalion: A Study of the Hermetic Philosophy of Ancient Egypt and Greece*. New York, NY: P. Tarcher/Penguin.

2 Foundation for Inner Peace (1992). *A Course in Miriracles,* Temecula, CA: Foundation for Inner Peace.

By Anna-Karin Bjorklund, M.A.

www.DreamGuidance.net

Crystal Souls

Goodnight!

Made in the USA
San Bernardino, CA
13 April 2016